Gimnastic

COLORING BOOK FOR GIRLS

Aisha Rang

In dance, every emotion finds its expression.

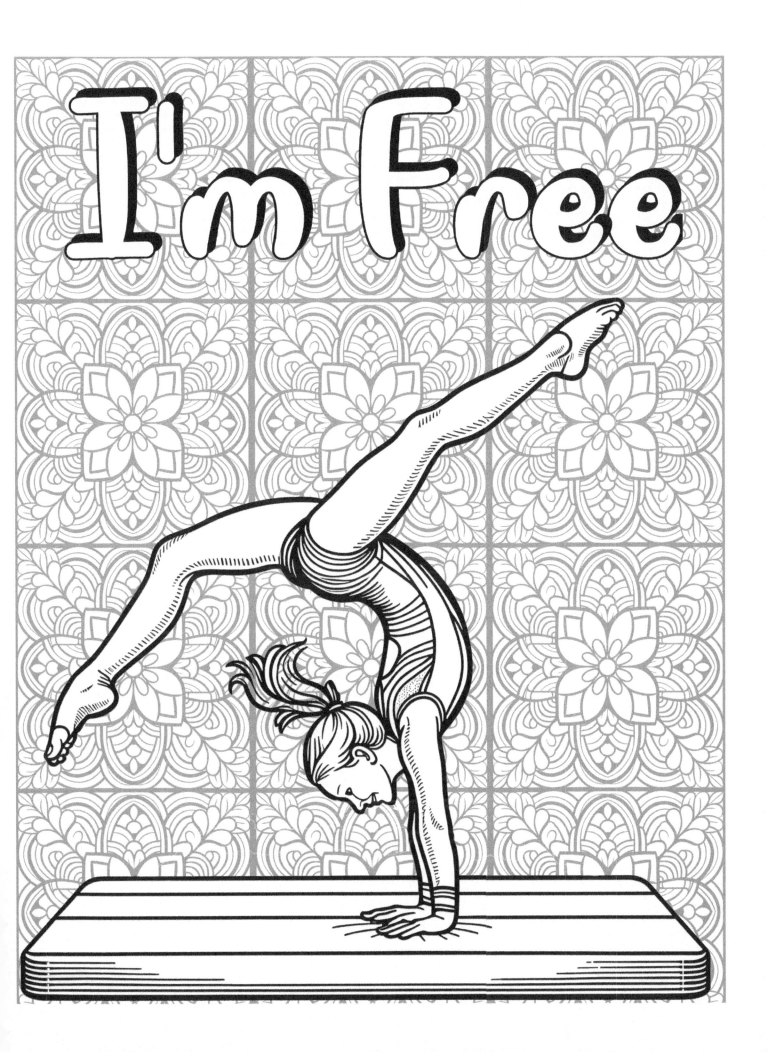

Flying is possible

with

effort

and passion

When you dance, every worry fades away

Face the beam with courage, conquer the podium with passion

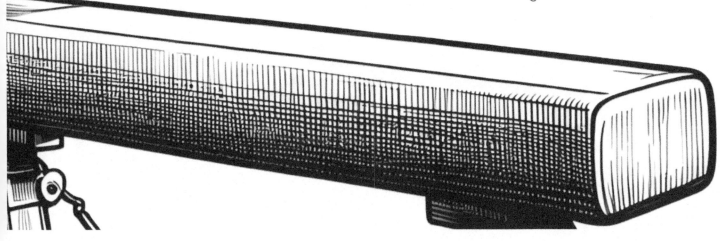

Be bold in your movement

free in your spirit

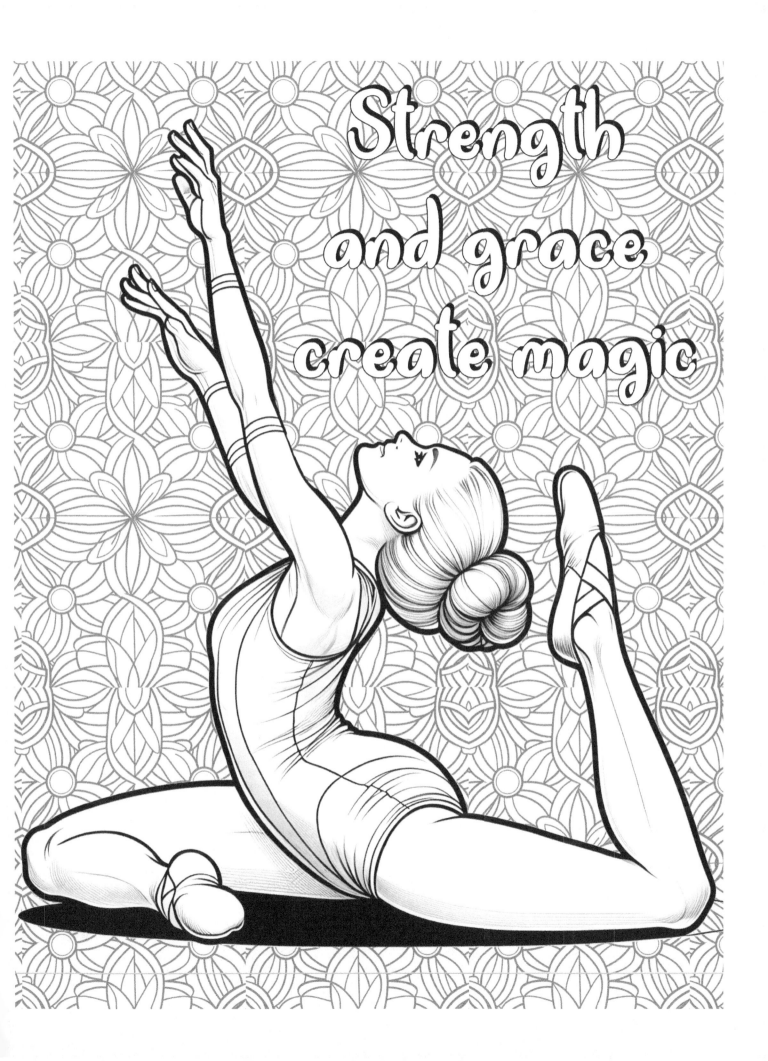

Dance with the soul

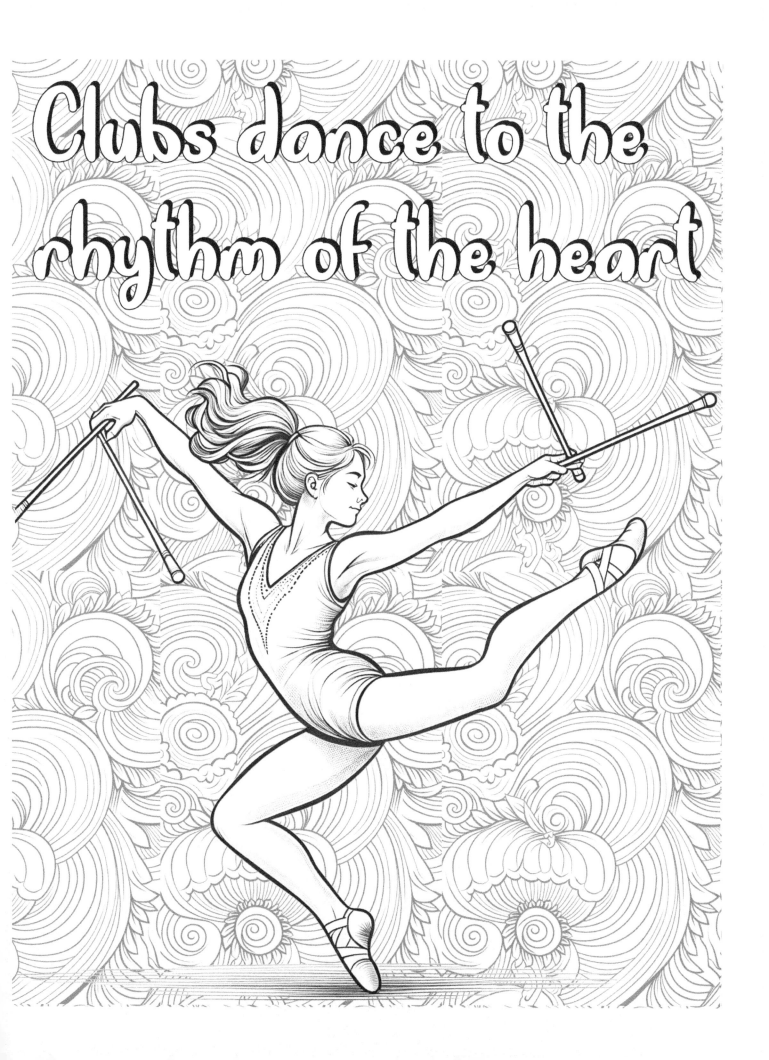

Each jump,
a challenge overcome
every routine,
a dream realized

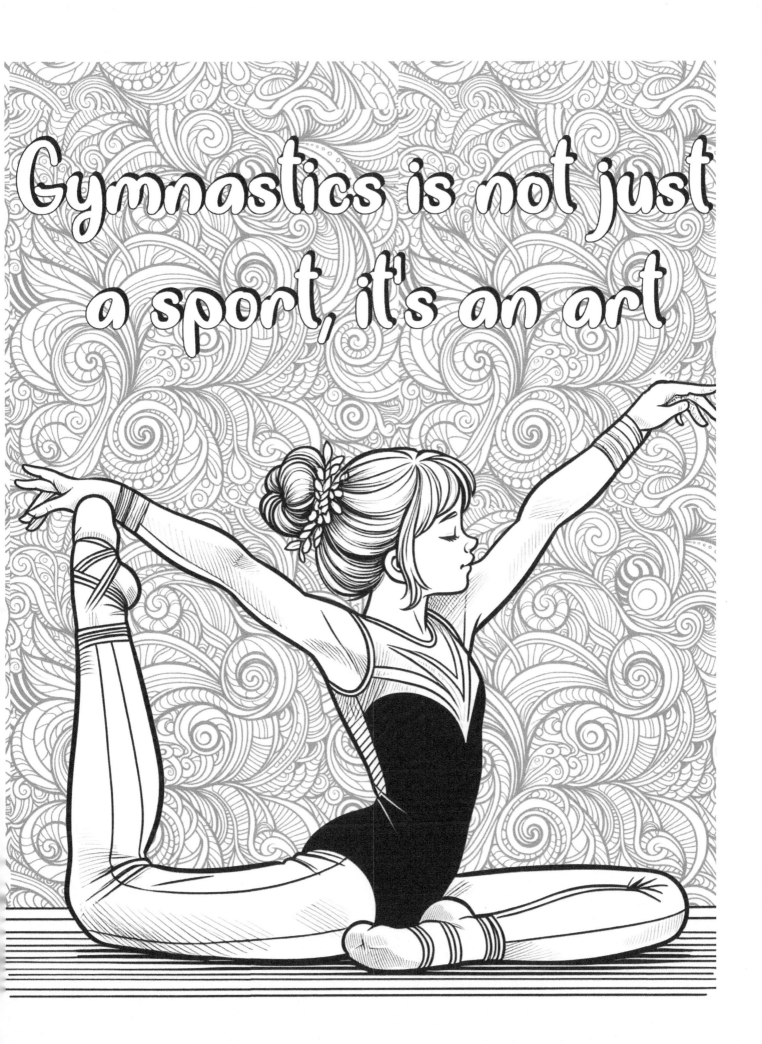

Embrace every challenge with a smile

With grit and grace, every dream is possible.

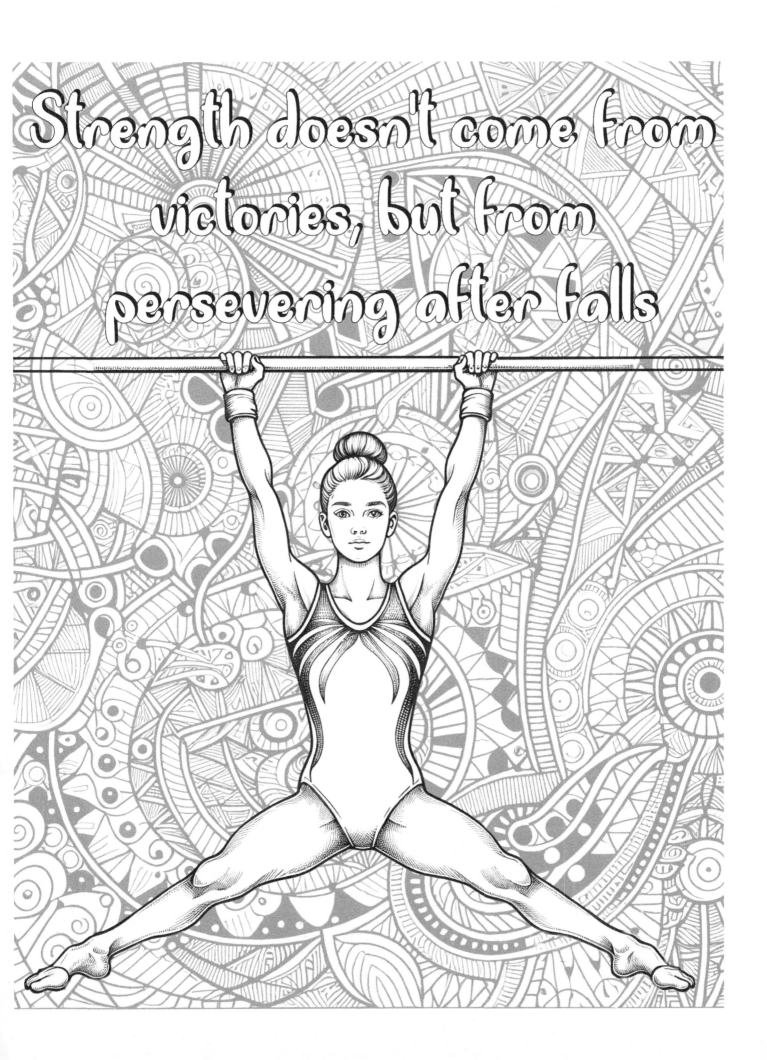

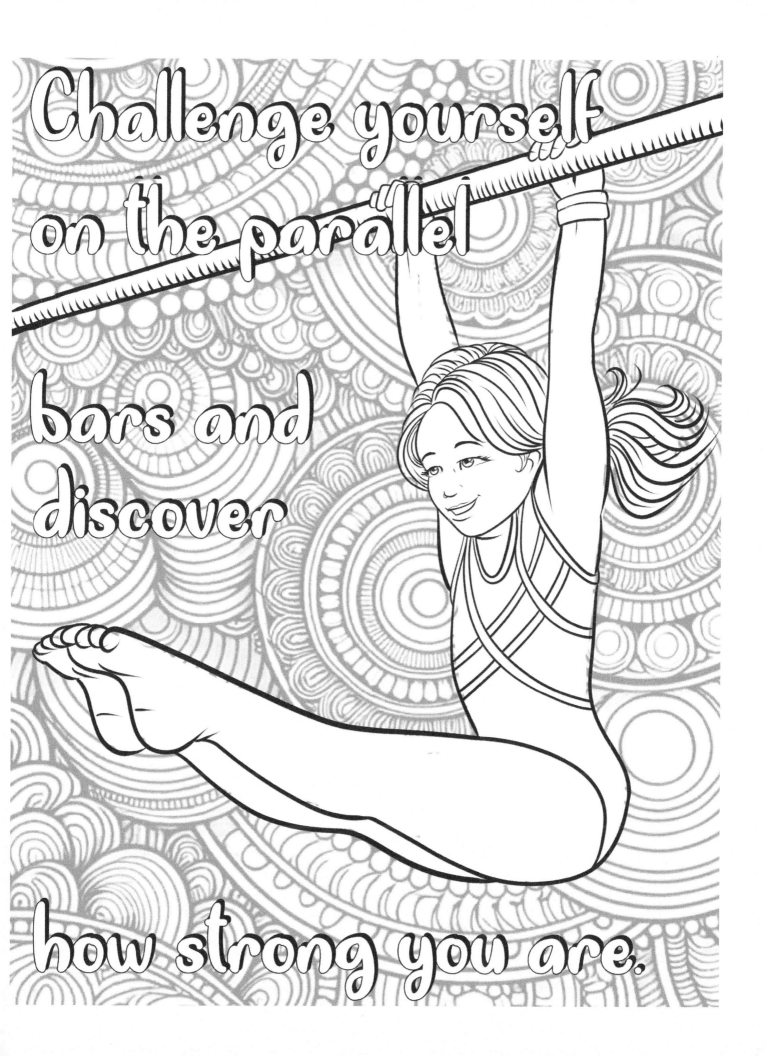

Made in the USA
Las Vegas, NV
18 April 2024